SHORT REFLECTIONS

Introducing "Macho Poetry"

Poems by

Louis Brown

ᴧA

Vabella Publishing
P.O. Box 1052
Carrollton, Georgia 30112
www.vabella.com

Manufactured in the United States of America

Library of Congress Control Number: 2014903981

13-digit ISBN 978-1-938230-69-1

10 9 8 7 6 5 4 3 2 1

This book is dedicated to the people of the Bremen Library who gave me more encouragement than anyone.

Macho Poetry

I call this "macho poetry" because pure poetry just doesn't describe how I write. Now the love poetry that I write is where I indulge my romantic side but I still choose to be simple and readable.

When I graduated Georgia State University I chose to go straight into the U.S. Paratrooper Department and later I moved to the Ranger Department. Then I attended college later in my life and people were a little surprised when they found I had a bent toward poetry. However, I have been writing all my life whether songs, poetry or stories.

I write down to earth poetry 97% of the time. I don't like my readers to have to try and figure out what I am saying. So I just call it "macho poetry", straight words from a man. I hope you like it.

Table of Contents

Love
Section I

Love and War

You understand

Your enemy in war

You know they mean

To shoot between the eyes

But lovers tear

Your whole world apart

After they've disarmed you

With a smile

Lyrics for Bianca

There's a woman in my arms
As close as skin can get
I want to fall in love again
I'm still not ready yet
Your shadow slips between us
Like every other time
And as cold chills cool the passion
Her love can't cross the line

My arms are full of memories of you
I pull the shades and lock the doors
But yesterday comes through
As I hold her in the dark
I still hold you in my heart
My arms are full of memories of you

I found her at an upscale dance
She's all woman to the bone
But I slipped and cried your name again
And I knew the night was gone
She slipped right through my fingers
Cause her pride can't play that role
She wants all of me or nothing
But it's not in her control

CHORUS

Yesterday Warmed Over

Today is where it's at the wise men say
Tomorrow's where it is for many men
I spend my time believing in another day...
Yesterday warmed over again

Some folks say I'm only wasting time
But love like ours is just too good to end
So I keep believing it's the only way...
Yesterday warmed over again

> I JUST CLOSE MY EYES UNTIL I SEE HER
> COMING AROUND THE OLD FAMILIAR BEND
> SPEND YOUR TIME BELIEVING IN TOMORROW
>   AND TODAY
> I'LL TAKE YESTERDAY WARMED OVER AGAIN.

She ran away with someone new in town
Too full of life to stay and love one man
But when she left she left my life another day...
Yesterday warmed over again

CHORUS

The Old Magnolia Tree

Beneath the old magnolia tree
I used to hold you close to me
And there I carved upon that tree
That I loved you and you loved me

Beneath the white magnolia blooms
You cast a spell with your perfume
I believed those wooden words were true
Ingrained in hearts of me and you

But time wears out what boys engrave
Nothing's left of the love you gave
Except that old magnolia scar....
I wish our love had come so far

Yeah, I wish those words were still on track
Cause every spring I dream me back
To tender lips and sweet perfume
Beneath the white magnolia blooms

But time wears out what boys engrave
Nothing's left of the love you gave
Except that old magnolia tree
Reminding me..... Reminding me..... .

I Found a Letter

I found a letter in an old coat pocket

I thought of you before my brain could stop it

It's been a long time healing

But I felt the same old feeling

Living in an old forgotten pocket

I found a letter yellowed by the ages

Your fragrance there came wafting from the pages

That memory stirs a dream

Much too bitter to redeem

All we had belongs now to the ages

I found a letter in an old coat pocket

A thought of you was there--I couldn't block it

In my old winter coat

The chill was in your note

I squeezed it into trash but couldn't drop it........

An Old Temptation

Temptation's bridge

Still stretches through the darkness

Tonight I'm sure

To cross it one more time

I long to feel

Those pretty lips slip open

A warm sweet push

Inside the curves I wind

I can't resist

The touching tenderness

The longing aches

That multiply desire

Where shadows arch

To peaks of rising pleasure

In sweet sensations

And waves of endless fire

That's why I go

Back to the nights that were

Always predictable

With feelings that were real

And you are there

To reward me one more time
To relive golden moments
Incredible to feel

Or I could go
Into the empty future
Where passion never goes
Not much there to gain
It can't compare
To that old bridge to darkness
That prism in my memory
Where pleasure knows no pain

The Right Decision

Pride tells me

I don't have to knock

Upon your door again

'Don't have to compromise

And let you win

It won't be hard

To learn to love again

But love tells me

No other's laughter

Takes my cares away

Like a miracle

Your magic makes me stay

Without you Girl

How could I find my way

Truth tells me

No man is an island

Unto himself

I'm lucky I found one

Who takes my breath

One who makes me

Bigger than myself......

In The Evening Rush

In the evening rush
Where frowns go past
I saw her smile
Eclipsed too fast
I turned around
And looked once more
I couldn't see
That warm rapport
So every day
I search that block
And pray she'll pass
At five o'clock
Those bright warm eyes
That rattled me
Have raised high hopes
So suddenly
A fire was lit
As my heart skips
Imagining
Her pretty lips
I long to see
Her cheeks turn pink
I sense she'll feel
The thoughts I think
I'll hunt her down
If that I must
Forever in
The evening rush

Time for Saying Goodbye

Fussing and fighting--that's all that we do
It's not worth the pain--this life puts us through
Let's face the facts...no late alibis
Baby, it's time for saying goodbye

At this old crossroad one path will be mine
And some feelings I have may last a long time
But our differences now ...are hard to deny
Baby, it's time for saying goodbye

Repeat
We were too young...it's all turned to pain
I don't see a rainbow in all of this rain
And if not much is left--there's not much to die
Baby it's time for saying goodbye

We had it all--Or that's how it seemed
But time changes hearts and life changes dreams
It happened to us--but we gave it a try
Baby it's time--for saying goodbye

Repeat

Bridge:
Still, teardrops may fall for way too long
But for closure we'll write us a helluva song.....

Repeat

Ice Age of 2013

I saw the sun go out

Your smile turned upside down

And cold blue eyes

Brought chilly silence

To this ice age

Where one more dinosaur

Became extinct

I've been a dinosaur

In other times

When love came by

I had a mentality

With Paleolithic limits

To understand

Female mystiques

It Was Many Springs Ago

It was many springs ago

That she'd light up my path

But what hurts deeper still

Is how many glaciers

Will melt away and then

How many fading stars

Will go icy cold and end

And how long Creator

Oh tell me how long

The eons will drag so slow

How many harsh winds will blow

Before she lights my way again

Women Are the Greatest People Going

Some women hook you with a wee bikini
Still they're the better gender of the breed
They don't start a war in far off places
They're gentle in their souls and in their deeds

They always make their men feel more special
And though they have their sprees at the mall
When you feel her wrap her arms around you
You know you're the one who's got it all

    Women are the greatest people going
    Their heart upon their sleeve is always showing
    She'll give you her last crumb
    My mother, she was one
    Women are the greatest people going

One can make my heart beat like a hammer
And leave my soul more peace than I have known
There'll be no World War III if you heed her
She's got a lot of wisdom in her bones

CHORUS

Bridge: Good mommas train their boys to grow up nice
       We'd all be kinder people if we took her advice
CHORUS

The Main Things

The clearly good

The obviously pure

The valued things

Deserving to endure

Avail themselves

With crystal clarity

To those who think

With love and charity

The Exit Sign

That freeway exit sign
Still leads to yesterday
Though it's better not to turn
Temptation has its way

There's our old house still there
I know that back bedroom
In love's finest moments
We helped the baby boom

A new name's on the mailbox
Love died one jobless year
That exit sign still points the way
But you can't get there from here

Catalyst

My love can make
My problems small
A piece of cake to handle
My love can light
An all night fire
With just a little candle

And in her arms
The smallest kiss
Turns winter into spring
But in her ire
My summer day's
A cold and hopeless thing

Chemical Attraction

The river's so wild

We may never cross it

The chasm's too deep

And too far

Love's a blessing or curse

For better or worse

I'm ready

Whenever you are.....

Valleys of the Moon

Old man they say there's magic
In your friendly face above
They say your smile can turn the tide
And inspire a human love
So I prayed you'd sprinkle moondust
On her sweet lips soft and warm
So when I get to kiss her
The kiss could last till dawn

But your old smile is only
Valleys of the moon
If lovers give you credit
I hate bursting their balloon
For her love would be all mine
If your magic was divine
Your smile is only
Valleys of the moon

Your skills are just a legend
Tied to that old cratered face
If you could cast a spell on her
I would know her warm embrace
But those asteroids that carved your smile

Were just an act of chance

You couldn't help me reach her

You know zero of romance

For your smile is only

Valleys of the moon

If lovers give you credit

I hate bursting their balloon

For her love would be all mine

If your magic was divine

Your smile is only

Valleys of the moon

Music written by Dawn Diamond

Silver-Tongued Devil

she asked

is there love

at the end

of the line

are the words

from your heart

or your mind

are they warm

empty phrases

or a pledge

for the ages

is there love

at the end

of the line

I Gave It To You

When I think of you I think of a smile

That shines from a long time ago

You were not ready to take on forever

I was...I fell at hello

Now I look inside for somebody new

For soft eyes that connect to my soul

With sweet lips so tender I ought to surrender

But I walk away in the cold

YOU WERE THE ANSWER TO ALL OF MY PRAYERS

BUT THE DREAM WASN'T MEANT TO COME TRUE

AND I CAN'T FIND ANOTHER TO GIVE MY HEART TO....

BABY, I GAVE IT TO YOU

All of my night dreams go back through the ages

To that warm and remembered embrace

A long living memory will roll down my cheek

There are some things you never replace

Chorus

Bridge: I'm still warming over your kiss

            But I know there's no future in this

I Remember You So Many Hearts Ago

Tomorrow's still a hill to climb

My new loves fade and die

They're so much like the seasons

Just hello and goodbye

But I can still remember one

Through yesterday's old mist

The love that time cannot erase

The sweetest on the list...

I remember you so many hearts ago

I can't give up the dream we used to know

Other hearts that I have touched were easy come and go

But I remember you so many hearts ago

I loved it when your lips were mine

Your shadow on my wall

When I pulled you close to me

I know we had it all

I never can forget you

I tried in every way

I find that each tomorrow

Begins with yesterday

I remember you so many hearts ago

I can't give up the dream we used to know

Other hearts that I have touched were easy come and go

Oh, I remember you so many hearts ago

Whistling By the Tombstones

As a boy I whistled in the dark
Walking by those tall tombstones
When I'd glance at that old graveyard
Frigid air would freeze my bones
As a man I've never been that scared
Till I saw your closet bare
I felt like that boy at midnight
Seeking courage with a prayer

I'm whistling by the tombstones again
Since I hurt you and you left me
I can feel that icy wind
I'll never make it through
Tomorrows without you
I'm whistling by the tombstones again

In my mind I miss your pretty face
And my backbone feels a chill
I tremble like that lonesome boy
Passing cemetery hill
If you don't come back it's darker
Than those graveyard fantasies
Cause it's just a grim tomorrow

Unless your dreams including me

So please don't say that little fuss
Could end our fairytale
All my life I'd be whistling down
Life's long long lonesome trail

I'm whistling by the tombstones again
Since I hurt you and you left me
1 can feel that icy wind
I'll never make it through
Tomorrows without you
I'm whistling by the tombstones again

Yesterday...

Thoughts of her and I'm back home

So happy to be there

I'll pull her tresses free

And stroke her long soft hair

I'll linger kissing her

And pull her warm and close

Time stands still one more time

On that old moonlit coast

It's surer than tomorrow

As I've learned she's kissed another

But yesterday...

We'll always have each other

In Love's Afterglow

I remember the beginning
And how you took my heart
The way your arms would hold me
Your lips so warm and soft
The way you bit my neck
To grab my full attention
And off to wilder tempos
Till love relieved our tension
We'd relax a moment
In lovers' afterglow
And soon you'd be right back
And off again we'd go
You woke my sleeping senses
And warmed me to the bone
Our loving was fantastic
With thunder in our loins
Just like two thoroughbreds
We pushed our outer limits
Holding back just barely
To delay the final finish
Milking all the sweetness
As hungry lovers might
To reach another pinnacle
Before the morning light

The Gentle Part of Me

I've looked at star filled skies

At life in microscopes

I've stared at hills and oceans

To find connectivity

But I have found

I see You clearest

Not looking past this skin

For You're the best in me

When I see gentleness

Like giving of myself

Being kind to others

Helping weaker ones I see

Caring for older beings

Showing youth the paths

And scorning selfishness

I see that love must be

His modus operandi

That is what I recognize

When everything is said and done

He is the grains on sandy beaches

He is the fish beneath the sea

He is the galaxy afar

The very tiny microbe

Everything I see

And finally

Whatever else

God is love in me

True Lies

tonight I started

believing my old lines

like I want you girl

I need you girl

until the end of time

it was different with you

the words were really true

there's nothing like

lying in your arms

Till the New Wears Away

Let us love

As long as it feels right

Even if it fades

In the morning light

Even if it lasts

Forever and a day

Let us love

Till the new wears away

This Could Take Forever

I felt it when I kissed you
Like lightning struck the air
Thunder rolled inside our hearts
At our introduction there
And passion was a wildfire
Everywhere you touched my skin
My heart skipped so many beats
A thousand dreams rushed in

And this could take forever
I can feel it
The farther into you
The more I need it
I discover some new side of you
Each night that we're together
Oh Baby, Baby
This could take forever

You bring love on many levels
How much is there to know
I'm peeling past the layers
Learning secrets as I go
There's beauty on the outside
And as I believe it's true
There's goodness and a lust for life
Everywhere inside of you ....

The Memory-Go-Round

too often I go

to the fair long ago

where there's laughter

and teardrops with music

the bright colored horses

ride circles

the calliope plays

where I blew it

where we rode together

and I look back forever

with memories of lips

sweet and soft

and a dreamer

still hates to get off…

Love Helped Me Grow Into a Man

Her gentle love would guide me
At the time I first appeared
From that big slap on my bottom
Through a lot of growing years
She could look pretty tall
With that hickory switch in hand
Her love helped me grow into a man

Later at a football game
A young beauty cheered our team
When she offered me a ride I said
"Don't pinch me--let me dream"
From the first time that I kissed her
My heart was in her hands
Her love helped me grow into a man

While the road from boy to man can be fantastic ...
Some angels have to work a little magic

She was twenty inches long
When her mother cried in pain
The doctor smacked our baby girl
And, ohhhh, she raised some cain

But she got a whole lot quieter
When I held her little hand
Her love helped me grow into a man

A man grows some each season
Till he's all that he can be
From a mother's care, through a love affair
To the last but not the least
They all were sent from heaven
And it worked out like He planned
Their love helped me grow into a man

A Loyal Man Indeed

I've always looked at dancing girls.
I think that all men do.
I drool at scenes
Like tight blue jeans–
Until they fade from view.

Where pretty girls are showcased
I'm sure to raise a toast
Cause a derriere
Might make me stare
Till I become a ghost.

And, yes, it's like a candy store
When beauties crowd the beach
Because a teeny
And snug bikini
Make my right and left eyes meet.

For I lo-o-o-o-o-ve to goggle long long legs
Whereever I may roam
And if they're cute
I will weigh the fruit
But I always boogie home

Religion

Section II

Hill

When hills are on my mind
I think Mt. Everest
Where snow caps brush the sky
Up past the eagles nest

Some feel desire to go
To climb the Matterhorn
Some love the history
Of the seven hills of Rome

But there's a hill much better known
It's not beautiful or high
Not famous for its ruins...
But one condemned to die

They say God's Son was there
And that lonesome road was hard
But He gave His all for man
And He made us sons of God

Alaskan Love Affair

I came to you, oh mighty land

Asleep to everything at hand

Lethargic from more southern air

Not yet awakened, unaware

The panorama I beheld

Composed a view unparalleled

A pastor with his best endeavor

Could preach forever and forever

And never say with words as clear

As the aura of this atmosphere

In the awe inspiring craggy peaks

And the chasms as His silence speaks

Where His creation stirs conviction

That brings a balming benediction

To one that hungers for a proof

Here, upon the planets roof

sons of god

as you programmed us all

to meet the challenges

no mountain is too tall

no ocean is too deep

no star can be too far

not one limitation

did you impose on me

and all I have to do

is take it on myself

invested with your power

as I confront each task

with knowledge here

of faith's unfailing strength

I know to persevere

to find a way

to think as gods

and do

Someone May Be Watching

Some child may well

Be looking up to me

If I stumble

They'll be there to see

I gotta walk the walk

Talk the talk

Be all that I can be

Some child may well

Be looking up to me

How To Move Mountains

When mountains are between me
And goals I must achieve
I have the strength to equal
How strongly I believe

However great the challenge
The evidence will prove
A dream with hope and shovels
Will make the mountain move

Homeless

I passed one who slipped
through the town's safety net
he stood in the drizzle
he might be there yet

the guilt in my heart
is not hard to explain
in god's love no brother
is left in the rain

Roses Don't Ask How

You know the truth

Already in your heart

Intuition

Has all answers

From the start

As roses

Don't ask how

They just bloom

Upon the bough

Be still

And truth unfolds

Within your heart

I Stand By in Awe

I stand by in awe

When beings live this life

Not lipping Bible verse

But doing kindly deeds

No mindful that their God

May ever reimburse

God Found Himself

god is here

god is there

in the trees

in the air

in the oceans

in the dew

in the mirror

howdy do

Teach Me

Teach me, My God.

To live with pain

To see the sun

Beyond the rain

To wear a smile

Through this lifetime

To show no fear

of hills I climb

Not that I ask

For special care

Give me the trials

That I should bear

I only ask

Lest others fall

That they see how

To stand up tall

Life

Section III

Old Ghosts Still Love To Dance

In that great big fancy ballroom
When that place is dark at three
There are two transparent shadows
On the floor you barely see

They are moving to the music where two spirits love to touch
In that scene they come together just like when they had so much

    Old ghosts still love to dance when life is gone
    They don't give it up; they just go on
    They can't seem to refuse it
    Cause they just love to do it
    These ghosts still love to dance when life is gone

Their nights are quite a pleasure but the cemetery beckons
They rush back home to weathered stones and fill two crypts in seconds

Just an ancient ritual...
Never hurt the town at all
And when mortals bring the music
They go and have a ball

    Chorus

Old Macon Road

I wander down

Old Macon Road

The countless years unreeling

I love the taste

Of yesterday

Reliving every feeling

I wander by

The old home place

To gaze through cracked old panes

The laughing ghosts

Are looking back

As it begins to rain

A sudden storm unleashes

And the memories

Fade once more

Just a house

With falling clapboards

As winds blow off a door

I wander down

Old Macon Road

As I have done so often

Now back to sleep

Till Gabe' s ole horn

In my old rusty coffin

Neglected Area

Where jungles stood
Great cities rise
On desert wasteland
New farmland lies
Where man aspired
To rearrange
He dreamed a dream
And made a change
His mind is such
A shaping force
You wonder why
Man treads a course
Indulging pride
Enslaved to greed
For inexorably
They lead
To mercenary depths
So deep
His God must sit alone
And weep
As man improves
Each varied part
Except for his
Primeval heart

Mission to Accomplish

Sometimes

We are like an army of ants

Marching forward doing God's bidding

Stepping on faces

Resolute and yearning to succeed

Though multitudes of us

Will fall by the way

But barely slowing the many

Relentlessly persevering

To fulfill the Master Plan

And nothing will stop us

Nay!! Nothing!!!!

Er-r-r-r by the way

Oh Creator.....

Where we going?

Another Side of the New Year

the bells

will ring out now

the horns

will make a din

and I will

laugh it by

but laughter

will belie

the tears

suppressed within

to see

the old year die .....

Love the Present

Love the present

This fleeting second

Indulge in the beauty

Of the flavor

The vision

Life's beautiful sounds

The fragrances

And focus on the dalliances of love

For all the sweetness of the moment

Capture the full rapture

Of the awakened senses

Freeze the panorama

That you may remember

In full sound and color…

It cannot pass this way again

Cycle

with life's first breath

the newly born

cries out in fear

for what could be

and at the end

with life's last breath

the dying man

goes out in fear

for what could be

Great Grand Paw Died at the Battle of Atlanta (Based on a true Story)

I'm going AWOL at first light

Sherman threatens my hometown

I hate to leave Robert E. Lee

But my heart's not backing down

There's a railroad to Atlanta

I'll fight side by side with Paw

General Johnson's too outnumbered

But we'll stand at Kennesaw

I don't like to leave Virginia

But Atlanta needs me there

With my family in danger

It's a duty I must bear

I'll meet Mayde at Big Shanty

We can have some time at last

I'll get up at the crack of dawn

And kick old Sherman's ass

Now I know we're way outnumbered

They have more than two to one

And Sherman hates all rebels

He's Abe Lincoln's favorite skunk

If we could get old Stonewall
To come down for just a spell
We could kick old Abe's invaders
From Kennesaw to hell

Mayde, I'm real scared of dying
If our rebel line should fall
But I'll stand to fight damn Yankees
Make 'ern think they hit a wall
We own no slaves but Sherman thinks
It's rebel killin' time
So I'll shoot holes in Yankee coats
Before there's one in mine

Why Men and Women Made It This Far

my nature craves a female

a female aches for me

so programmed for each other

the male one and the fe

oh sweet reality

Tribute to Jockey Wiggins

I once knew a guy named Jockey

A kind and noble friend

Trueblue and full of loyalty

Trustworthy to the end

Predictable I guess you'd say

Not one to let you down

A wise guy not unto the least

Just great to have around

Good humored with comradeship

He loved his fellow man

With not a mind for finding fault

More with a helping hand

A finer guy I've never known

And there's no truth to bend

I'm glad that I can always say

I'm proud he was my friend

Love in the Stars

We're on our way to the Milky Way

Far from a memory

There's nothing in my yesterday

As good as what I see

This woman's got it all for me

Our skin feels like one

Flying through eternity

I hope we're never done

This new angel's in my arms

Has set my spirit free

I finally found a love so warm

No room for memories

There's all I could desire

The imagination's sweet

We're fulfilling every dream

In our fantastic treat

Tonight we'll look for Venus

Where there's two cloudy moons

Make love on misty satellites

Between two sandy dunes

Speed around the cosmos
In a perfect flight so rare
So close to you I know
You always take me there

We'll pass the great big dipper
I'll drink a toast to you
The constellations will fly by
Till Terra Firma's due
My feet will stand upon our world
My mind still high in space
I've never gone so far with love
Than here in your embrace

Appraising Eyes

I'm sometimes in the limelight
Not by my own request
But there are young observers
And I must pass their test

They'll be evaluating
The character they see
And some of them may imitate
The side I've shown of me

So let the smile be friendly
This helping hand no less
And let my legacy be one
Of having shown my best

A Dark Windy Serenade

The wind plays a music that swells my despair

Paints darker the setting of my lonely lair

Where I would recover from dreams kicked aside

My eerie tormentor comes back like the tide

Whistling and keening from high pitch to soft

Stirring the pigeons awake in the loft

Screeching a branch on my window of stars

Playing the drainpipe in monotone bars

Resting and racing then altering course

"I saw your loved one" says its haunting voice

Routing the season of flowers and sun

Clearing the path for a desolate one

Going All the Way

Man moves real mountains

Conquers deep oceans

Explores new infections

While probing the stars

With God in his spirit

He tackles the mysteries

for answers beyond us

It never occurs

To doubt His Great Maker

Who opens new trails

To far away worlds

Out far past forever

And then turning inward

As worlds microscopic

Shrink smaller and smaller

Finding new questions

The farther he goes

It seems not to end

In stars or in atoms

Amazed that forever

Keeps going both ways

Back to a Town

I came back to a town
In a year of my life
To nothing the same as before
I thought I would capture
All the familiar
But time had barred shut every door

I came back to a town
The first haven I knew
I never would see it again
Like Mr. Wolfe said
Nobody finds it
It's gone just like yesterday's wind

I came back to a town that nurtured and reared me
Forgot me, not one hand to hold
And there was a man there
In all the shop windows
So utterly lost in the cold

Do It Now

The thing

That we have to remember

Our moments

Are precious and brief

Old time

Is a hammering ocean

And life

Is a vanishing reef

Hole

We are random shallow creatures

Doing as our God programmed

Seeking answers so elusive

Working hard like cosmic ants

Keeps faith but never knowing

When new hope will come in sight

Always stumbling through the darkness

Then the future turn hard right

Heading for a vortex spinning

Down and down a hole so black

Until the boundaries are full

And pressures start to pushing back

Overstraining the compression

Till inevitably the blast

And as millenniums go past

Slowly, finally resurrection

In a tiny blade of grass

Finally Connecting

Imagine what
No finite mind can gauge
Count the countless years
Millenniums and miles
We had to cross
To meet

Imagine here
This fateful rendezvous
Ordained before the stars
Before old Sol
Above us there
Was christened blue

Imagine now
To culminate a love
That came so far
And finally
The merging here
Finally…

Alien Birthplace

The neighborhood is gone

Familiar faces

Nowhere to be seen

Portland cement hides

The dusty street below

As progress left its scars

Razed our shotgun house

And poured an interstate

The corner gang is gone

So precious few,

Can be accounted for

They are the ones

Who lie so still and cold

Beneath incongruous slabs of stone

With names of barefoot friends

I used to know

Final Encounter

He waits in ambush

Down the road of time

Around some bend

Atop some lonesome hill

That black highwayman waits

To do his loathsome task

Inexorably,

The road draws closer

To this abomination

Who waits to pounce

Some tired misfortunate

Whose time runs out

I cannot dodge his keen

And bloody scythe

I'll be trembling

Perhaps wailing with remorse

On this untimely day

At odds with my demise

For before I go

I hope to frequent

All the taverns

Quaff the potent elixirs

And dance with all

The dark eyed girls I can

To test each proven pleasure

Invent a few myself

Until I know for sure

I've had a chance to taste

The last sweet drop of life

Before that final rasp

They Call Themselves the True Church

They come meekly, humbly

To build their New York mosque

In peace and feigned love

And then in time they change

And when their power is grown

They tell you they are real

The true church of the world

And those who will not join

Are lowly infidels

An insult to their god

Without a right to live

Their armies come

just like in centuries past

And cut off heads

Of non-believers

Do we want them here

In free America

To mutilate our girls

And make them less than dogs

They made a killing ground

One day on 9/11

When Islam spawned hatred

Blew our towers to dust

And Americans splattered pavement

Oh how they danced with glee

From Karachi to Tehran

In time they dream to dominate

From Maine to Key West

From Georgia to L.A.

With hate filled ancient laws

The code of Sharia

Shoved in our passive faces

Well, as for me

They can shove it up

Their camel sweaty asses

I say go to hell

You ignorant aberrations

But don't come here

We need no more of you

You murdering bastards

(I came to know a promising young man who was murdered in
the Twin Towers on September 11,
2001)

Wisdom Comes and Goes

Should I still stretch

For new proverbs

And hope

They never age

While old truths fade

Each epoch's dawn

And worms digest

Each page

Wisdom From Your Heart

When I don't have the answer
to a problem in my path
and I want to help my neighbor
show some love on his behalf
I'll find words of wisdom
and an answer with some art
'make sure my intuition
comes directly from my heart

For it's shaky ground to walk on
if no guidebook's written yet
when words are loosely spoken
there's reactions to be met
and I'll need a wise solution
with the words that I impart
for words are more enlightened
if it's wisdom from my heart

So I'd say it's more than muscle
that sends life thru every vein
it's the organ I believe
where your better angel reigns
it's the station that He tunes to;
there's no equal counterpart
and you'll know you're on His wave length
when His wisdom fills your heart

Thank You Mr. Heston

Ring up the deaths

From sticks and stones

And slingshots

Knives and clubs

T.N.T.

And nuclear bombs

Their total sum

By year 2010

Counts fewer deaths

Than guns

The chosen tool

That beats 'em all

North and south

East and west

Guns can't be outdone

Say thank you NRA

And get your gun

Opportunity

within this span
of fleeting time
i weigh the marrow
in your bones
exalting courage
most of all
i see your steps
from dawn to dawn

rich or poor
i watch you pass
black, white, or tan
i do the same
let mankind know
my door swings wide
let anyone
enrich their name

though i am proud
to see you grow
i must require that you fulfill
one vanity
that i may know
you seek me out
with fervent will

I Am an Anglo

I am an Anglo

Pondering the Indians again

I know we won that war

I recall my greedy ancestors

Exiled them to reservations

Out west for the rest

Of their history with white men

I find no joy in cruelty

Punishing vibrant people

Pushing them off their land

Just because they forgot

To get their deeds

Recorded at the courthouse

They owned it first

It was their real estate

And they had the right to hunt

These hills and vales

Forever in God's eyes

Until we drove them out

Stealing every vital acre

As we called them savages

So it would look all right

To abuse them and take

Their world from under them

We shoved them all

Along the trail of tears

And other paths

While the savages for real

Are the ancestors

Of the people

Whose faces we see

In our mirrors today…

Slow Learners

Beyond this time and place

Reviewing epochs past

We will recall this phase

As just a stumbling step

Toward fuller consciousness

As we evaluate

The values taught

The goals we sought

The strange pursuits

We tried to mesh

When men bypassed

The quest for truth

For greeds

Of finite flesh

The Old Chain Swing

Her boy went off to war and died
A long long time ago
Now nameless under foreign turf
She half forgets it's so

Out in the yard an old chain swing
Still holds a rusting board
And with each gentle breeze that blows
Swings of its own accord

On sunny days she sits alone
And peers at empty air
Without regards to laws which say
That no one could be there

As though she still can hear a shrill
Of laughter from the swing
She smiles toward the swaying board
Immune to time's swift wing

Moment of Truth

There is a past age

That no one can alter

And tomorrow will be

What tomorrow will be

But here in the middle

Is one precious moment

A quicksilver instant

That challenges me

Honesty 101

It's up to me to build the future
With commitment in my heart
Being honest with my neighbors
Is the point where I must start
A life must always aim for truth
No hypocrisy prevail
With no blemish in my make up
If I aim for less I fail
Integrity to one another
Puts a deeper trust in place
To uphold that awesome value
Is to lift the human race
I must always stand on honor
And be forthright to the bone
Always strive to be less selfish
Where no evil turns me wrong
There will be a better future
On that loftier plateau
God will bless me for the wisdom
If I choose that course to grow
When I truly ply those basics
There's a difference I can make
I must be a good example.....
Our third planet is at stake

Once Upon a Hobo (A True Story)

I knew the man who stole more miles

Along the southern rails

Fifty-five years he rode those trains

On plains and mountain trails

I don't know what possessed my kin

If running from or to

But he loved those long freight trains

The only home he knew

It wasn't that he cared so much

Where those big wheels would roll

It was always in the going

That satisfied his soul

You couldn't tie my cousin down

On icy days or warm

A whistling train was in his thoughts

The day he bought the farm

I'm very sure what Heaven's like

For that old pal of mine

It has to be a long long freight

On a long long railroad line.....

Humor

Section IV

Waffle House Romance

That pretty blonde waitress
Who brought my morning coffee
In that unbuttoned blouse
Is gone today

She had me leaning forward
To watch her bending low
As she poured out her best
All just for me

It seems she took great care
To keep me coming back
For Colombia's mountain grown
And for the canyon view

Some coffee breaks are long

Big Girls Are Truly Wonderful

They're warm

In the winter

Darn good

With a splinter

And far better chefs

Than the men

They're sweet

And sincere

They look great

From the rear

I'd like

A nice harem

Of ten

I Never Went to Bed
with a Real Ugly Woman

I never went to bed

with a real ugly woman

It's just the proud man deep in me

Close as I came--

one had her teeth stained

But her heart was as pure as could be

I never went to bed

with a real ugly woman

It's just something I never would do

If I passed out from gin

does it count at the end

If I did, er, wake up with a few.....

Yesterday's Gone
And Yesterday's Here

I walk my hometown street where everything is gone
Looking for my girlfriend, who I did so wrong
A few familiar faces...but most just disappeared
And yesterday's gone but yesterday's here
In my heart

I pass the old shop windows where I see my self
Coming by to ask again how long she's been left
Nothing is quite the same in this old atmosphere
Cause Yesterday's gone but yesterday's here
In my heart

    I guess yesterday's my strangest fascination
    Tomorrow just can't catch my imagination
    It's because she gave me all I'll ever need
    Lord...I know that yesterday's my speed...

It's a ghost town full of lonely ghosts
If I'm not one, I know I'm pretty close
I left her many times; neglected her for years
Now yesterday's gone but yesterday's here
In my heart

    Chorus

Statue in the Park

I must warn

The high achievers

To stop reaching

For the sky

Great success

Has its downside

Over rainbows

Do not fly

If you do

You'll get what's coming

Oh, you'll stand tall

In the park

But you'll always be

The target

Where the pigeons

Leave their mark

The Sad Short Life of Marvin

There's many little dramas
That you never hear about
And I have one to tell ya
That will really wring you out

The highway streamed with traffic
And Marvin Moth loved beams
His growing curiosity
Was reaching the extremes

Luminescence caused a rapture
In this creature with his wings
He was only a beginner
And so fearless of such things

Uncle Fuzzy said, "Don't go"
His Mommy said, "Stay here"
But Marvin thought he knew it all
And he shifted up a gear

He told himself, "Oh goodness me,
That must be where "it's" at
When he puckered up to kiss it

I don't guess he heard the SPLAT!!

So I doubt he ever suffered
But I shudder through and through
Every time I see a headlight
With a smudge of gummy-goo

DON'T GIVE TOO MUCH

Give your neighbor all you can
Give sweat unto your boss
Give your troubles to the wind
With just one mighty toss
Give your kidneys to caffeine
A hundred years they'll go
Give Gene Simmons your big butt
And let your skinny show

Give your payments to the bank
To send your kids to college
Send 'em to a better school
To give their noodles knowledge
Give charity to old goodwill
To prove your heart is pure
Like Robin Hood take from the rich
And give it to the poor

Give tithes unto your preacher man
He'll get you through the Gate
Throw in a golden nugget
You may not have to wait
One last thing Mr. Houseman adds
Give carefully your hearts
Give crowns and pounds and guineas
But don't include your arse

Shadows in Love

our shadows

come together

on the wall

they must think

we still

have it all

just this final night

and we'll be gone

one last time

for the good times

we have known

They don't know

It's the final curtain

That it's over now

Except the hurting

Cause our silent partners

never had a fuss

they're still

having fun

being us

Opposites Attract

Life's river's so wild

We may never cross it

Temptations lure us

But the chasm's too far

Love's a blessing or curse

For better or worse

I'm ready

Whenever you are

Over My Head

There're mystic poets

I figure not

And why does thunder

Bring rainbow arcs

When God passed out

Fine minds galore

I must have been

Behind the door

For with galaxies

And inner depths

I'm overcome

With so much breadth

Too much to grasp

And penetrate

There's just too much

Upon my plate

My data base

Should be much greater

My wee gray matter

Won't hold the data

Not Quite Shakespearean

Once upon a century

I typed in Microsoft

Testing metaphors

For new profundities

Much like the caveman did

Many centuries past

I strived to find a way

To scribble on a wall

Some moving exposition

In Century Twenty- One

I hammered mine on bond

With Brother script

To say something cool

That Shakespeare

Or his ghostwriters

Never put to pen

And finally

Wrapped it up

Did my wall

And left my card

Eat your heart out

O William the Bard

On the Wildhorse Dance Floor

She's so beautiful

She makes my goose bumps tall

I've gone from lonesome

To a man who's got it all

The night's so good

I may never be the same

I'm so deep in love

Maybe I should ask her name

Man Has Two Strikes Against Him

How can You criticize the beast

You made with Your two hands

And fault him for his foibles

When he disrupts Your plans

He can't escape his drawbacks

His skills and mind are weak

Before he bit the apple

He could have used a tweak

He only feeds the hungers

You programmed in his brain

He has two strikes against him

It's almost inhumane

We're dumb to kill each other

But You sowed every seed

So take him back into Your shop

Perfect him to succeed

You can't expect that much

From nothing but a dunce

If You can see the future

Please get it right for once

My First Airplane Ride;
My First Parachute Jump

They put me by the door

And I could see below

800 feet to the ground

A solid green carpet

Looking soft enough to sleep on.

But the limbs underneath

Were sharp and deadly.

It wasn't a good day

For a jump I thought.

Who wants to jump out of a C-47

On their first airplane ride

Into the wild blue yonder--

No one with good sense

As I answered my own question.

I remembered hearing about

The guy who received a parachute

Not knowing it needed repair

But he had faith nothing happened

To a nice guy like him.

So when he jumped out

And didn't feel the jolt slow down

His descent to the ground

He looked up with panicked eyes

And saw the chute fluttering away.

He muttered a few cuss words

When he saw the ground come fast.

He didn't pull his reserve in time

And never heard the deadly thud.

Those were my thoughts

As the T-7 parachute

Opened with the snap of a whip

Just as the parachutist behind me

Started walking on my canopy.

I could see his boots sink in deep

And I hollared, get your sorry ass off

You low life no good bastard--

A panic lingo that flowed out

Because I was scared crapless

At the turn of events.

Luckily my chute didn't collapse

And his chute started floating away.

No harm done except my nerves

Were a little frayed.

It only takes about 8-10 seconds

To get to the ground

From the time you leave the plane.

So I looked down and there it was

With the wind blowing about 20 knots.

I could feel myself swaying

Much like a pendulum on a clock.

I wasn't trained to land on my back

As I'd learned the five point landing technique

But then the ground slammed my rear

With a sledge hammer effect

Knocking the light off in my brain.

But I must have awakened shortly

As the wind had opened my canopy

Dragging me across the rocky landing zone

Till I became aware and remembered

To pull the bottom risers on my chute

To empty the air from it

So I could roll on top of it.

Then an instructor came by yelling

Get your ass up soldier

And take your chute back where you got it.

I responded accordingly

Wanting to keep my nose clean

And make the rest of my jumps

So I could get my Parachutist Wings.

It would take 4 more jumps that week.

I had to meet those requirements

Or they would send my derriere oveseas

Where a war was going on.

That was all the incentive I needed

To bust my butt gladly

And claw my way to paratrooper status.

Geronimo-o-o-o-o-o-o-o

I thought sheepishly to myself

For my not so altruistic bravado.

www.ingramcontent.com/pod-product-compliance
Lightning Source LLC
Chambersburg PA
CBHW061148040426
42445CB00013B/1617